Edwin D. Morgan

Governor's Message

Edwin D. Morgan

Governor's Message

ISBN/EAN: 9783337811488

Printed in Europe, USA, Canada, Australia, Japan

Cover: Foto ©Suzi / pixelio.de

More available books at **www.hansebooks.com**

IN ASSEMBLY,

January 7, 1862.

GOVERNOR'S MESSAGE.

To the Senate and Assembly:

In the presence of events so momentous as those now surrounding us, we can but realize that man's strength is weakness, his wisdom foolishness, and human forecast a mockery. It is most fitting, therefore, that we seek the favor of the great source of all power and knowledge, and implore the counsel of Omniscience in our deliberations. Let us remember that from devastation and bloody strife, God restores the wasted land and evokes peace; while from a condition of apparent prosperity and mutual faith, He may permit the spirit of discord to enter, and suddenly bring a whole Nation to the verge of humiliation.

In communicating to you the condition of the State, I acknowledge with feelings of the profoundest gratitude the blessings of Almighty God in preserving the public health, in rewarding the labor of the husbandman, in prospering the great industrial and commercial interests, and saving the popular mind from all tendencies to disorder. But beyond our beloved State, truths, the most painful, force themselves upon us. Abroad, those nations whose friendship

we have for generations cordially cultivated and desired,
whose rights we have scrupulously observed and whose sym-
pathy we had expected, have turned coldly upon us in our
trials, and with a perversity that causes more of sorrow
than of anger, will not understand the vital questions un-
derlying our difficulties. At home, the year 1861 has been
the most eventful in the annals of the American Union
and of constitutional freedom. It has just closed on a
great nation, torn by Civil War, and threatened in its very
existence. The calamitous strife that has marked it has
deepened into tragedy, and the present year opens at a
period big with interest to ourselves and consequences to
our posterity.

Without stopping to consider antecedent facts, we behold
a rebellion of extraordinary proportions, menacing the
safety of a government, whose common benefits have made
us a free and prosperous people, and given us an honored
name in every land and on every sea. A vast army alone
keeps back this beleaguering tide, saves the national capital,
protects the persons of the lawfully chosen Chief Magistrate
and his constitutional advisers, and preserves the public
archives.

New York has been no idle spectator of the progress of
the insurrection. She responded to the first summons
to protect the endangered Capital, and to-day one hundred thousand of her brave sons bear aloft the banner
of the Union, in and near the rebellious States. From
her imperial resources vast supplies have been drawn for
the war. Her bankers, and particularly those of the city
of New York, with a patriotism and an enlightened confi-

dence, which is a wonder to Europe, and a marvel to ourselves, have furnished a most important element to the government. She has freely contributed from her public treasury, as well as in the cities and towns, through formally organized action of private citizens, and through the less formal means of individual benevolence. The care of the families of Volunteers has been assumed by municipalities, by villages and by individuals. The cord of brotherhood has been strengthened by our public grief, and this dire calamity has afforded the American people a sad opportunity to vindicate themselves from the calumny of national selfishness. The spirit of universal liberality and fraternal kindness will everywhere be accepted as convincing evidence of the moral integrity of the people in this hour of trial, of unalterable attachment to their institutions, and determination that not one jot or tittle of national rights or dignity or manhood shall be surrendered. The commanding position of this State, never so obvious as in this struggle, renders her voice potential in a great crisis like this. For the time being, you are to give utterance to that voice. I am sure it will be no uncertain one.

During the year the administration of justice and the execution of the laws have been prompt and universal. Our State credit, an index of abiding confidence in the Government, never stood higher than now, and though drawn upon for the war, our finances, as will appear from the exhibit which I now submit for your consideration, are in a satisfactory condition.

There was in the Treasury, on 1st October, 1860, $3.299,537 49
Received from all sources for the fiscal year 16,942,977 53

$20,242,515 02
Payments ------------------------------------ 17,167,573 17

Balance on September 30th, 1861 ------------ $3,074,941 85

The debt of the State, on October 1st, 1861, was:

Of General Fund Debt--------------------- $6,505,654 37
Of Canal Debt----------------------------- 26,081,610 25

Making a total of ------------------------ $32,587,264 62

The Stock or Funded Canal Debt outstanding on September 30th, was authorized by the Constitution as follows, viz:

	Principal.	Annual int. of
Article 7, section 1	$9,739,024 76	$532,341 48
do 7, do 3	13,200,000 00	782,000 00
do 7, do 10	642,585 49	34,629 28
do 7, do 12	2,500,000 00	150,000 00
	$26,081,610 25	$1,498,970 76

During the last fiscal year, that portion of the Canal Debt recognized by section one, of article seven, of the Constitution, has been reduced by the payment of $982,974.23 of the principal from the constitutional Sinking Fund, arising from the canal revenues. It will be further reduced before the 30th of September next by the redemption of two million, one hundred thousand dollars of maturing stock from funds applicable to that purpose; leaving due, after that period, a principal of twenty-three million nine hundred and eighty-one thousand six hundred and ten dollars, and twenty-five cents, with an annual interest thereon of one million three hundred and eighty-one thousand, nine hundred and seventy dollars, and seventy-six cents. An average annual reduction, past and prospective, of more than one and a half million of dollars, is thus shown; and

4

it is confidently believed that the stock, amounting to seven million seven hundred and thirty-nine thousand and twenty-four dollars, and seventy-six cents, maturing previous to January, 1871, will be met as it falls due from the surplus revenues of the canals set apart by the Constitution for that specific purpose.

Years of taxation and disappointment in relation to the cost and income of the canals, will give to the exhibit presented below more than usual interest. This shows a gain in the Canal revenues of nine hundred and eighty-six thousand and thirty-nine dollars, and ninety-one cents, and at the same time a reduction in the expenses of forty thousand one hundred and ninety dollars, and sixty-four cents, making a total net gain over the past fiscal year of one million and twenty-six thousand two hundred and thirty dollars, and fifty-five cents.

Revenues:

From tolls on the Erie canal	$3,020,153	31
Champlain canal	106,561	00
	$3,126,714	31
Oswego canal	131,458	38
Cayuga and Seneca canal	18,778	32
Chemung canal	15,319	04
Crooked Lake canal	699	94
Chenango canal	23,397	24
Black River canal	6,112	73
Genesee Valley canal	29,189	60
Oneida Lake canal	218	86
Baldwinsville canal	22	57
Oneida River improvement	919	63
Seneca River towing path	190	38
Cayuga inlet	147	97
Total from Canal tolls	$3,353,168	97
From rent of surplus water	4,865	00
From interest on current revenue, &c.	44,594	33
	$3,402,628	30

Expenses:

Payments to superintend'ts for repairs	$106,611 51	
To contractors for repairs	260,995 33	
To Canal Commis'rs for repairs, &c.	224,957 28	
To collectors for salaries, clerk hire, pay of assistant collectors, inspectors, and expense of collectors' offices	62,345 55	
To weigh masters	8,111 30	
For salary of Auditor and clerk hire in Canal Department, salary and extra clerk hire of State Engineer, refunding tolls, printing and miscellaneous payments	43,765 17	706,786 14
Surplus revenues		$2,695,842 16

The revenues have followed the direction contemplated by the Constitution, which is in order as follows, viz:

1st. To pay the expenses of collection, superintendence and ordinary repairs of Canals, as above	$706,786 14
2d. Transferred to Sinking Fund under article 7, section 1st of the Constitution	1,700,000 00
3d. Transferred to Sinking Fund under article 7, section 2 of the Constitution	350,000 00
4th. The remaining surplus transferred to the Sinking Fund under article 7, section 3, of the Constitution	645,842 16
	$3,402,628 30

CASH STATEMENT:

Balance in the Treasury and invested on the 30th of September, 1860		$2,375,017 76
Received, viz:		
For canal tolls, rent of surplus water, interest on revenue, &c.	$3,402,628 30	
For proceeds of loans and premiums	1,216,883 50	
For proceeds of taxes	840,552 28	
For miscellaneous	145,183 84	5,605,247 92
		$7,980,265 68

Paid, viz :

For redemption of stocks........	$2,175,551 23	
For interest on stocks	1,505,304 64	
To Canal Commissioners, repair contractors, superintendents, collectors, and weighmasters.....	1,626,821 76	
Miscellaneous	67,966 80	
		$5,375,644 43

Leaving a balance to the credit of the Canal Fund on the 30th of September, 1861, of.....		$2,604,621 25
Of this balance there was on deposit in banks to the credit of the Treasurer on account of the Canal Fund.................	$2,435,845 04	
Of investments held in trust by the Auditor :		
Bank Fund stock................	37,743 15	
New York State and Canal stock.	106,880 00	
Of real estate securities :		
Walter Joy's Bank..............	20,354 06	
Bank of Corning...............	3,799 00	
		$2,604,621 25

Of this balance, the sum of four hundred and eighty-nine thousand, five hundred and thirty dollars and twenty-nine cents, was not available, it being the aggregate of the canal deposits in insolvent banks; but, since the first of October, a portion of this amount has been paid into the treasury, and it is estimated that the ultimate loss on deposits in suspended banks will not exceed two hundred thousand dollars. Since the termination of the fiscal year and up to the close of the calendar year, the revenue from canal tolls was one million nine hundred and eighty thousand four hundred and ninety-seven dollars and forty-nine cents, the expenses of collection and repairs about two hundred and nineteen thousand and sixty-two dollars and sixty cents, and the available balance in the treasury and the several deposit banks on the 1st instant, was three million nine hundred and fifty-one thousand four hundred and twenty-seven dollars and forty-seven cents.

By the opening of navigation the enlarged canal will be completed throughout its whole extent. The circumstances of the country are such as to give to this fact its highest importance. To those Boards, Commissions and State officers whose duties have connected them with this work, and with operating the canals, the people owe their thanks, and especially so to the Canal Board and the Auditor of the Canal Department. The completion of this work should lessen the engineering expenses in an important degree. The system of contracting for repairs of the canals is found to materially decrease the yearly expenditure, but the structures become deteriorated, and at the end of no inconsiderable period the State will be obliged to make good the annual depreciation by new structures at large cost. I would therefore recommend that such change in the law, governing the letting of canal repairs, be made as shall require that no sections be let without giving notice by advertisement, and the contractor be required to give ample security that he will leave his section in as good condition as he found it; and further, that every section be inspected by the proper officer when it is surrendered, and any depreciation be enforced against the contractor.

The railroads have seriously diverted business from the canals. The extent of this is most marked in westward-bound freight. Of the revenue of three million nine hundred and seven thousand six hundred and seventy-seven dollars, received during the last navigation season, only two hundred and eighty-three thousand two hundred and seventy-two dollars were collected at the cities of New York and Albany, and at West Troy and Waterford, on freight bound westward and northward, while the tolls at Buffalo and Oswego on freight eastward bound were two million seven hundred and five thousand eight hundred and twenty-three dollars, or nearly twelve times more. There can be no question that the carrying of merchandize, which forms the bulk of westward freight, is almost exclusively enjoyed by the railroads. In 1851, before tolls were removed from railroads, there were three hundred and sixty-five thousand tons of merchandize carried on the canals, paying eight hundred and seventy-seven thousand dollars in tolls, while in 1860 there were but two hundred and fifty thousand tons transported, paying only two hundred and twenty-three thousand dollars, or a reduction of nearly seventy-five per cent. This results from no diminution of this class of the carrying traffic, for the annual report of the State Engineer and Surveyor on railroads will show that the business of the railroads has largely increased in the transportation of merchandize. In 1851 the tolls on merchandize formed thirty-five per cent. of the revenues of the canals; in 1860 it was but seven and one-half per cent.

To make the business of the canals depend so exclusively on the products of the forest and vegetable food, is to assume the largest risks. The carriers of merchandize have an assured business even in seasons of partial crops, of low prices or fluctuating markets, but that means of transit whose business is restricted to transportation in a single direction of coarse staples may, by a contingency, find its traffic reduced below the cost of the service. While our canals will always be large carriers, yet undue competition may divert their legitimate business in desirable traffic to such an extent as to disqualify them from meeting their constitutional demands.

The largely augmented revenue of the canals, while due in a degree to increased tonnage, is principally owing to the enhanced rates of toll. Although much effort was made to reduce the tolls, yet the Canal Board of 1861 wisely retained the schedule of 1860, increasing the rates on some articles. There may be periods when rates unfavorably affect the business of transportation on the canals; it is certain that last year was not one of these, neither do I believe the present year will be. Experience conclusively shows that reductions in toll, although made avowedly to retain to the canals the business which might fall to other modes ot transit, result in loss of revenue. It is clear that our true policy lies, not in the direction of striving for employment at unremunerative prices, but in protecting the canals in their legitimate business, and demanding proper tariffs for their use. In what manner this shall be accomplished, I have endeavored to point out in former messages. After presenting these facts, I can most safely leave the important question to you, who have so recently come from the people and know their views.

The General Fund Debt remains unchanged. The principal is six million five hundred and five thousand six hundred and fifty-four dollars and thirty-seven cents. The annual interest thereon is three hundred and sixty-seven thousand eight hundred and twenty-seven dollars and fifty-eight cents, of which three hundred and fifty thousand dollars is chargeable by the Constitution upon the General Fund Debt Sinking Fund; but owing to the temporary inability of the Canal Fund to pay into the treasury, from its surplus revenues, this sum to the Sinking Fund, the interest for four years preceding the last was paid from the General Fund revenue. Last year the increase in the Canal revenue was again sufficient to meet this obligation. To the Legislature of 1861, for the first time in a quarter of a century, the Comptroller was enabled to show a balance to the credit of the General Fund; and the considerate policy, in the main, of the Legislature of last winter in regard to appropriations, enables me to state that a balance of fifty-three thousand seven hundred and fifty dollars and fifty-one cents, stood to the credit of this fund at the close of the fiscal year ending with September last.

The State tax of three and five-sixths of a mill, levied in 1860, has been paid into the public treasury. The net amount was five million three hundred and ninety-seven thousand five hundred and twenty-four dollars and forty-five cents. This sum includes the ordinary levy of a million and sixty-four thousand dollars for schools, and two million seven hundred and fifty-one thousand dollars for the Canal Fund; the remainder is for the support of government. The Legislature authorized a direct tax of four and three-eighths mills for 1861. Of this, three-quarters of a mill was for schools, three-quarters for canals, seven-eighths for general purposes, and two mills for defraying the expenditures under the Act authorizing the embodying and equipment of a volunteer militia, and to provide for the public defence. Anticipating an instalment of forty per cent. from the Federal treasury upon the advances made by the State (which has been received), the Comptroller, to whose discretion the question was left by law, caused the levy for war purposes to be reduced to one and a half mills. The direct tax for the present year will therefore be three and seven-eighths mills on each dollar of the taxable property of the State.

The defects in the assessment laws are found to be such as to throw more than three-fourths of the burden of taxation upon real estate. This is evidently unjust. The whole property of the State, personal as well as real, should be made to pay its due share of the cost of government. As such is not now the case, the importance of a revision of the statutes relating to assessments is manifest, and especially so at this time, in view of the large prospective taxation to be apportioned by the General Government to this State, required for the expenses of the war, and which is laid only on real estate. Our laws relating to the assessment and collection of taxes were, in the main, enacted nearly a half century ago, when property consisted mostly of lands. The amendments which have been made from time to time have been so imperfectly drawn that, by resorting to expedients, the owners of personal property have been enabled to escape taxation. In some of the States, taxpayers are required to make sworn inventories of their personal property. It remains for you to say whether or not this mode, or some other equally efficient one, shall be adopted in this State. The manifest partiality shown to personal estate should at once engage your attention. The annual report of the State Assessors, presenting their views on this subject, together with tables of valuation and other important exhibits, will be early communicated to you; and to that I refer you for valuable data. From this it will appear that the total valuation of real estate in 1861 is $1,121,134,-480, being an increase of more than $1,000,000 over the preceding year; while a decrease of nearly $7,000,000 in valuation of personal property is shown.

In this connection I feel it to be my duty to allude incidentally to the subject of the extension of time for the collection of taxes, and to respectfully refer to my former annual and special messages in relation thereto; time and experience having strengthened and confirmed the opinions therein expressed.

The acts of April 14th, 1860, and April 17th, 1861, in relation to capital punishment should be repealed, with a careful saving as to all offences heretofore committed. If not repealed they should be essentially modified. Questions of the most serious importance have been raised in regard to certain provisions of these Acts. There is evidently a settled purpose in the public mind to divide the crime of murder into two grades, only the most heinous of which to be punished with death. This change has my decided approval, and would, I believe, serve to meet many of the objections to existing laws. A law should be passed containing a new definition of murder in the first degree, confining it to poisoning, killing by lying in wait, and killing where there was a deliberate design to effect death, formed by the accused prior to the meeting between the accused and the deceased on the occasion of the assault that proved fatal. This would exclude all constructive murders and render punishment more certain. Aside from all other serious objections, the definition of murder in the first degree, in the Acts to which I have referred, includes offences involving no more moral guilt than the commission of an assault and battery. I commend the subject to your early consideration.

Last year I fully stated my views respecting the pardoning power, which subsequent observation has served to justify. During the year 1861 there were presented to me four hundred and two applications for pardon; added to this number were ninety-five cases undecided on the first of January last, and forty-seven applications for re-examination, and a total for examination of four hundred and forty-four is thus produced. Of these I have pardoned sixty-six; have denied four hundred and two; have commuted fifteen; discharged by court and terms expired forty-one; leaving twenty undecided at the termination of the year, in consequence of incompleteness of papers.

In 1861, I recommended the passage of a law providing for the appointment of a commission to inquire into the system of our prison management, with reference alike to discipline and economical administration. The Legislature, probably for want of time, omitted to take any action on the subject. Finding, in the latter part of the summer, that the duties connected with the raising and equipping of volunteers for the service of the General Government, were such as would prevent me from making my annual visit to the prisons; and in view of the fact that the derangement of the business of the country might ultimately cause, if it had not already produced, embarrassment in

the prison finances, and also incidentally affect the discipline
of the prisons, I deemed it advisable to request the Superintendent of the Albany County Penitentiary, whose long,
intimate and successful connection with penal institutions
peculiarly qualified him for the duty, to visit the State
prisons, to examine into their police and fiscal management, and to report the result of his observations to me in
writing. This he has done. I desired him to make suitable inquiries in regard to the alleged severity of punish-
ments inflicted at Sing Sing, and respecting the administration of the affairs of the Lunatic Asylum connected
with the prison at Auburn. I also requested him to make
such inquiries as would enable him to determine if the
recent murder committed at Clinton prison was the result
of any want of proper foresight, or of any insufficiency in
the rules or discipline of the prison. The result of his
examinations, though necessarily only partial, shows the
need of a commission of the character above named. As
will be seen below, the actual receipts are fully a quarter
of a million of dollars less than the expenses of the prisons.
This difference is increased of course beyond what it
would be in ordinary times, but is due in a great measure
to the mode of contracting the labor of convicts. I would
not be understood as underrating the ability or faithfulness
of the several officers to whose hands are confided the
general and local administration of prison affairs. They
have exhibited much interest and have put forth active
efforts to preserve order and to render the prisons produc-
tive; but the disciplinary and fiscal systems are of many
years' standing, and every test proves them to be very

faulty. It does not appear possible that able-bodied men, of ordinary intelligence, sentenced in every case for at least two years, and occupying quarters valued at more than a million and a half of dollars, should be unable to meet their support. The subject is certainly of a nature to invite the most scrutinizing attention. It is my deliberate opinion that, when the Constitution shall admit of the change, it will be wise to substitute for the three Inspectors of Prisons one Superintendent, to be appointed by the Governor and Senate, leaving to the wardens the duty, under proper regulations, of contracting for the convict labor and of controlling the government and internal management of the respective prisons.

Discipline, and reformation of the convict, are questions of primary importance in our prison system, and should engage the most serious attention. The subject of finances, though but secondary in comparison, is entitled, especially at this time, to the most careful consideration.

The total expenditure for the prisons during the last fiscal year, including forty-four thousand one hundred and seventy-nine dollars for building and permanent repairs, was three hundred and eighty-seven thousand one hundred and forty-three dollars and sixty-five cents. The amount of earnings paid into the State Treasury was but ninety-two thousand nine hundred and thirty-nine dollars and eleven cents. A large sum, however, remains due from the contractors for convict labor. Should application be made to you, too much caution cannot be exercised in entertaining the subject of releasing contractors. Serious injustice has heretofore resulted to the State from interference with obligations of this character. For details respecting commitments and discharges of prisoners, the special care and management of the prisons, I refer you to the annual report of the Inspectors.

The three prisons have recently been enlarged, and it is expected that no further appropriations for this purpose will soon be required.

It has been suggested that a small percentage of the earnings of convicts be placed to their credit, and paid them on their leaving the prison. There is good reason for believing that future crime would often be prevented, if this were done. Many of the discharged convicts are without friends, and nearly all of them are dependent upon the labor of their own hands for support. Not unfrequently, before procuring employment, or their good resolutions have acquired sufficient strength, their slender means are exhausted, and they choose unfavorably between beggary and theft.

The following is a statement of the number of convicts in the prisons on the 31st of December, viz:

Auburn prison	829
Auburn Asylum for Insane convicts	79
Sing Sing prison, males	1,277
Sing Sing prisons, females	135
Clinton prison	512
Total number	2,832

There were in the Asylum for Insane convicts, at Auburn, on the 31st of December, seventy-nine patients. With so limited a number of inmates, requiring a relatively large attendance of officers, the expenses of the institution, even with the strictest economy, will be proportionately large. In this connection, your attention will be called, in the annual report of the Inspectors, to a class of criminal insane, confined in county jails, whose mental condition deserves notice. I recommend you to make suitable provision for removing those of this class most seriously diseased to this Asylum, who, on the application of the district attorney, shall be ordered there by the presiding judge, to be treated at the expense of the respective counties.

The system of higher education in the colleges and academies of the State continues in uninterrupted operation; and, though the spirit of patriotism, always ardent in the schools, has withdrawn professors and students from the peaceful pursuits of learning to the defence of their country, the number of pupils has not been more reduced than it has often been by financial embarrassment in times of peace. In many of these institutions military companies have been formed, and the students have attained a high degree of perfection in military drill. This is especially true of the State Normal School. Its physical and disciplinary effect has been most salutary—in the former respect even superior to gymnastic exercises. I recommend that works on military tactics be introduced as text-books into these institutions, and that drill be made a part of the exercises. To enforce the observance of these requirements, the income of the Literature Fund should be awarded with reference to the proficiency and attention given to this branch of education.

During 1861, the aggregate attendance upon our common schools was about the same as for the year 1860. The expenditure for school buildings and improvements, is in excess of the preceding year. The deportment, health, and future usefulness of the pupils, in preserving and, if need be, in protecting, the institutions and rights of their country, would fully justify me in recommending that male pupils above the age of twelve years be instructed in the elements of military science for a portion of the year in all the schools supported at the public expense, provided it be practicable. It may be so in cities and larger villages; but in country districts, its feasibility is doubted. The subject is worthy your attention.

The building for the People's College is yet in progress. Numerous applications from this and other States have been and are still being made for admission. It is expected by the Trustees that all things will be in readiness for opening the institution next autumn.

The Annual Statistical Reports of the Secretary of State on pauperism, and on criminal statistics, will afford you valuable data on those two topics.

The Superintendent of the Banking Department will be able to present a very satisfactory account of his responsible trust. During the fiscal year there was a decrease of about $1,852,000 in banking capital, which at the close stood at $109,982,324. The aggregate of the securities held in trust for the free banks was $30,213,780.59, or an increase of $18,318; while the aggregate circulation issued to free banks was $28,360,482, or a decrease of $380,934. In addition to this, it appears that $464,661.32 in bonds and mortgages have been withdrawn, and government and state stocks have been substituted therefor.

Since the close of the fiscal year, about one million dollars in securities have been added, and the circulation has been increased between eight and nine hundred thousand. It will appear that six banks suspended during the fiscal year, with an aggregate capital of $1,464,560. The securities held in trust for their circulating notes were sold by the Superintendent, and all their outstanding circulation, with the exception of that of one bank, is in process of redemption at par. On this, with a circulation of $51,554, there was a loss to holders of seven per cent.

The Superintendent of the Insurance Department will submit a detailed account of the several insurance companies, located and doing business in this State. From this it will appear that, with a single exception, no failure of Fire, Marine or Life Insurance Companies has occurred during the past year.

The State Engineer and Surveyor will submit to you a report on the condition of the enlargement, and other matters connected with the canals; and also a report on the railroads of the State.

The inspection of salt at the Onondaga Salt Works, during the past year amounted to 7,200,391 bushels. This is in excess of any previous year. A duty on this production, at the rate of one cent per bushel, is payable into the treasury, and forms a portion of the permanent revenue of the General Fund. The expenses of the works, salaries of officers, and the cost of providing supplies of brine to the manufactories for 1861, were about forty-six thousand dollars. In his annual report the Superintendent will communicate information bearing upon the future of this important interest. I respectfully refer to my last annual message in connection with this subject.

The Superintendent of Weights and Measures has furnished me a carefully prepared statement of the articles and the condition of the public property under his supervision. From this it appears that all the counties of the State, with the exception of four, have been supplied, through him, with new or corrected standards of superior workmanship. The duties of this office are conducted with commendable economy.

There were landed of alien emigrants at the port of New York, during the past year, sixty-five thousand five hundred and twenty-one, against one hundred and four thousand three hundred for the year 1860. For the first four months of 1861 emigration exceeded the corresponding period of 1860 by several thousands, but during the latter half of the year there has been a large falling off; reducing the aggregate arrivals thirty-seven per cent. below the preceding year, and less than during any year since the organization of the Board of Commissioners. The reduction of income thus occasioned, has induced a rigid economy on the part of the Commissioners, who expect that, without detracting from the usefulness of the commission, they will be able to support the institutions under their charge without assistance, until emigration shall again enable them to meet the ordinary demands upon their income. The report of the Commissioners will be presented to you in due time, and to that I refer you for valuable details.

A floating hospital for the treatment of yellow fever is proven, I think, by the experience of the past three years,

to have advantages over fixed quarters. It is found to be
not only better for the comfort and well-being of the sick,
but safer and more economical. We can, therefore, at least
safely postpone the purchase of lands, or the erection of
costly edifices, or the employment of an expensive corps of
salaried officers, for quarantine purposes, until the political
troubles of the country are at an end. The report of the
Quarantine Commissioners will present the affairs more in
detail; but it is proper that I should call attention to the
necessity for a suitable site for a warehouse for infected
cargoes, as it is believed that this is the principal source of
danger from yellow fever. The cost ought not to be large,
as the requisite accommodations would be inconsiderable.
The Commissioners will endeavor to impress upon you the
necessity of a revision of the Quarantine laws. Authority
should be given to sell the grounds lately occupied as a
Quarantine station on Staten Island, and, in that case, to
provide for a new boarding station at a suitable point elsewhere; to require the proper distribution of the sick, and
to provide means therefor; to invest the Health Officer with
control over the Floating Hospital; and for the permanent
maintenance of anchorage ground for infected vessels in the
lower bay during Quarantine season. The office of Physi-
cian of the Marine Hospital, which, since the resignation of
the incumbent in June last, has been vacant, should be
abolished, the salary of five thousand dollars heretofore
paid should be saved to the emigrant fund, and the Health
Officer be required to perform the few remaining duties free
of expense.

The labors and responsibilities of the Metropolitan Police

have temporarily been materially increased by the quartering within the district of large numbers of soldiers, and by the passage through and detention in the city of regiments from this and other states. Additional duties were also imposed at the last session of the Legislature. Without display, however, and in a manner to win still more fully the popular confidence, the police have preserved the public peace and faithfully performed the duties assigned them. The annual report of the Commissioners is now in my hands, and will be transmitted to the Legislature without delay. It embraces a large amount of important detail, and contains several recommendations for your consideration. There is an increase of four hundred patrolmen in New York—a number amply sufficient to protect life and property, and to repress any outbreak against the public peace. Statistics are therein given with reference to the sanitary police, and the examination of unsafe buildings and steam-boilers (more than twenty per cent of which are found defective), and the mode of escape from and ventilation of tenement houses. The importance of frequent and careful examination of ferry boats plying in the harbor of New York, is established by the returns submitted with the report, which show that during the past year forty-four million six hundred and forty-one thousand eight hundred and ninety-five passengers were carried, with the loss of a single life, that of a fireman, while cleaning his engine. The Commissioners suggest the propriety of imitating European cities, in transferring to the police many duties now discharged by other functionaries, and thereby saving largely in expense while gaining in efficiency. The supervision of weights and measures, custody of the markets, inspection of streets, piers and bulkheads, and enforcement of laws for the government of the harbor, are those specially named. The duty of appointing poll-clerks cannot with propriety remain vested in the Board, but should be transferred to the supervisors of the counties. There are other points which will engage your attention. The standing of our State and country abroad depends, in no inconsiderable degree, upon the good order of the commercial metropolis, and a system of police which has proved itself, under trying circumstances and careful scrutiny, to be equal to the objects sought in its establishment, properly claims such legislative aid as experience has proved to. be requisite.

The Board of Commissioners of Pilots have continued to satisfactorily discharge the duties devolved upon them by the several acts of the Legislature relating to the preservation of the harbor of New York. In their annual report, they will call your attention to several important subjects connected with the wharves, piers, slips and waters of the harbor of New York.

The number of vessels of all kinds, arriving at the port of New York, in 1861, was fifteen thousand and sixty, exclusive of river craft. To insure the proper care of these, it is necessary that the several harbor masters should be continuously at their posts. Such, however, has not been the fact during the past year, but as there is no law expressly forbidding these officers from absenting themselves, or from employing persons to perform their duties in their absence, there exists no authority for correcting a very obvious wrong upon the commercial public. I therefore renew the following recommendation contained in my last annual message :

" I think some amendments are necessary to chapter seventy-two, of the Laws of 1850, relating to the harbor masters of the port of New York. The defect of the law is found to be in not prohibiting harbor masters from employing assistants to perform their duties and from absenting themselves from their posts ; and it is believed that these subordinates, to some extent, exact and receive illegal fees for berthing vessels. Stringent provisions against the employment of assistants under any pretext whatever, and against demanding, receiving, offering or paying gratuities, should be adopted."

The practical operation of the act of April, 1857, reorganizing the Board of Port Wardens, seems to meet with general approval. No change will therefore be necessary. The annual report of the President of the Board shows that 10,844 surveys were made for the year ending with the thirtieth of November.

Marked progress has been made during the past year in developing the Central Park, although the expenditure was but about one-half as much as for 1860. The condition of a portion of the work commenced in the latter year, required its completion in order that it might be saved from damage. The great utility and growing beauty of this grand municipal enterprise have already given it a high value in the estimation, not of New York alone, but of the public at large.

Benevolent institutions are springing up in every part of

our State, devoted to specialties.   There could be no better evidence of the humane tendencies of our people than is afforded by this fact.   Some of these have been instrumental already in accomplishing much good.   I would specially mention the Children's Aid Society, organized in the city of New York, for the purpose of providing homes for vagrant and homeless children.

The managers of the several charitable institutions of the State have reported to me their present condition, with a brief account of the administration of their respective trusts.   The New York Institutions for the Deaf and Dumb, and for the Blind; the Asylum for Idiots at Syracuse; and the Lunatic Asylum at Utica, have each been measurably prosperous, and I am glad to inform you that, with a single exception, they require no special legislation. As the usual annual report will be made to you from each, presenting a statement of its affairs in detail, I respectfully refer you thereto, for specific information.

In regard to these and all similar objects, seeking aid from the public treasury, I desire to repeat the following recommendations contained in my message of 1861:

" While the State should be exactly just, and while I should be unwilling to counsel a withdrawal of its patronage from the several charitable institutions which have hitherto enjoyed it, I would suggest the adoption of a more rigid system of accounting and economy with regard to them.   The doctrine of strict accountability should apply as well to our charities as to any other interest.   I am sure that no valid objections can be urged against this by those to whose hands the interests of these important

establishments are committed; since it will afford to the
people a satisfactory guaranty that the moneys appropri-
ated to those objects have a proper direction. I would
recommend that all applications for aid to State institutions, beyond that for usual and necessary support, should
be carefully scrutinized, for it cannot be denied, that while
their ordinary affairs have been generally managed with
care, large expenditures have sometimes been made for
mere ornamentation. If we keep constantly in mind the
fact that the taxpayer is charged with the care and support
of the poor of his own locality, and, in addition, willingly
pays all that is required of him for these general purposes,
applications for aid will be more carefully considered; and,
by limiting the amount only to actual wants, we may be
less liberal, but more just."

The New York State Inebriate Asylum at Binghamton
is not yet completed. The report of the officers will afford
some interesting detail in respect to the character of applications for admission.

The Society for the Reformation of Juvenile Delinquents,
in New York, will also present to you a favorable annual
report. Their buildings are completed, and the fullest
efficiency of the institution is now being enjoyed.

The Managers of the Western House of Refuge, located
at Rochester, will present you their report, showing a
very satisfactory condition of affairs at that institution.

The Department of Public Charities and Correction has
renewed to me the recommendations I made in my last
annual message, to which I respectfully refer, and which I
now repeat. The Commissioners very justly call attention

to the fact that no provision has been made for the soldier
who, after being disqualified, from wounds received in service, has returned to the State, without pension or means of
procuring proper medical attendance, and is left to depend
upon the charity of the public. Congress ought, at once, to
make suitable provision for this class of cases. Near the close
of the last session of the Legislature, a bill providing for
the more certain and guarded prosecution of vagrancy and
other petty offences in police courts in the city of New
York, was presented for my signature. Such of its provisions as were indicated by the title were proper and desirable, but in some other respects it was so objectionable
that I was unwilling to give it my approval. It provided
that the several claims of the police justices to make their
compensation equal to that allowed the city judge, should be
liquidated from the revenues and receipts of the court, and
be paid to them by the chief clerk of their own court;
and, further, the incumbents were to be continued in office
"until provision shall be made for their successors by
appointment or election, as the convention to amend the
Constitution shall determine." I was not willing to give
validity to an act which permitted a subordinate to receive
fees and compensate his superiors, without any check being
put upon his acts. Not only was there more than one subject
embraced in this bill, while but one was expressed in the
title, but it doubled the compensation of the police justices,
and made their official term depend upon a future contingency, which, as it might never happen, would give them
an unlimited claim to the office.

Agricultural interests have been more than usually prosperous. The products have been abundant throughout the State, and the remunerative rates have given increased business to the various modes of transportation in the direction of markets; at the same time the articles of human food have been so reasonable that plenty has been within the reach of the humblest laborer. Public policy alone would counsel us to foster this great source of happiness and national wealth.

I have heretofore recommended an enlargement of the powers of boards of supervisors. I believe that the public interest would be materially promoted by widening the scope of their legislative jurisdiction. But should this be done, I advise that it be coupled with a provision making it necessary, especially in counties where there are cities or large villages, to procure, before they can take effect, the approval of a designated county officer to all acts, ordinances or resolutions levying special taxes, or creating debts. It appears to me that, for several reasons, the county judge would be the proper officer to perform this duty.

I desire to call your attention to the necessity of at least two amendments to existing laws affecting the powers of supervisors and town boards: the one respecting the extension of time for the collection of taxes, when stayed by injunction; the other in relation to providing means for constructing bridges when destroyed by accident and for the extraordinary repairs of roads. As regards the former, it is shown by experience that the provisions of chapter 488, of the Laws of 1851 should embrace and be made applicable to boards of supervisors in cases relating to the imposition and collection of taxes, and that, after the stay of proceedings is terminated, a period not exceeding the number of days during which such stay or suspension continued, should, after their making proper return, be allowed to collectors. As respects the latter recommendation, it is only necessary for the Legislature to provide for calling a special town-meeting to vote upon the question of levying a tax or making a loan. In addition to this, it would be well to increase, under suitable restrictions, the amount now authorized to be borrowed by boards of supervisors. Each Legislature is obliged to spend much time, at serious disadvantage, in examining these subjects, often at the risk of legalizing debts whose propriety could more readily be determined by the voters or local officers of the districts directly affected, and especially by those persons from whom the moneys are to be drawn. At present, under the plea that the town elections have passed, and no power exists for calling the electors together, or that the sum now authorized to be raised by boards is insufficient to meet the exigency, the Legislature is induced to assume responsibilities which belong to local officers, to whom it should be exclusively confined.

A cursory examination alone of the subject will show that more than seventy per cent. of the counties are proportionately, and all are actually, wronged by the present system of paying the cost of transportation of state prison convicts, and the expense of executing writs of requisition, from the State treasury. I have heretofore called special attention to this subject, and now renew the recommendation that the cost be made a county charge. There can be no doubt whatever of the justice of this policy.

A change is obviously necessary in the laws relative to excise so as to ensure their enforcement, especially in regard to licenses. At present those who pay for licenses practically receive neither privilege or protection therefor.

I consider is unnecessary to repeat at length the views presented by me in former messages, in regard to the following subjects. I desire to say that reflection and observation have only served to confirm the propriety of the recommendations; and I therefore renew them: the conferring of larger discretion upon judges in fixing the terms of sentence of criminals; that aliens actually residing in this State be authorized to acquire, hold and convey real estate at their pleasure; that females convicted of crimes, involving imprisonment for a brief period, should be sent to the penitentiaries instead of the State prison; that a careful attention be given to the subject of public health, especially in the city of New York, and particularly to providing the necessary scientific sanitary supervision; that it be made the special duty of some officer to enforce the law of April 12, 1853, providing for the care and instruction of idle and truant children; that a revision of the laws applicable to breaches of trust in various forms, and to persons acting in fiduciary capacities, has become necessary; that power should be given to the Governor to suspend for misbehavior, during the recess of the Senate, all officers where removal or suspension is not otherwise provided for.

I would earnestly ask your attention to the subject of the modification or enactment of city and village charters. They are generally ill-digested, and, except in special instances, entirely unnecessary. A well considered act or some amendments to the general law of 1847, would be far better calculated to secure the objects sought in village charters, than such as swell the size of our annual session laws. On reference it will be seen that the subject of city and village charters occupies two-fifths of the space of the last annual volume of laws.

The Constitution has determined that no private or local bill shall embrace more than one subject, and that shall be expressed in its title. There is, evidently, a growing tendency to incorporate inconsistent provisions in local bills. This is clearly contrary to the spirit of the constitutional provisions. I respectfully ask your attention to this subject in making up the annual tax levy of the city of New York, and in other measures affecting the several cities of the State.

By the Act of the sixteenth of February last, the sum of $50,000 was appropriated for the purpose of furnishing supplies and provisions for the relief of the suffering people of Kansas. The Governor, Comptroller and Secretary of State were constituted a commission to superintend and direct the expenditure of these moneys. A competent agent was employed by them, who, under their direction, at once proceeded to carry out the provisions of the Act. A report on the subject, made by the commissioners, will be found in the last Assembly documents, number one hundred and forty. The sum of thirty-eight thousand seven hundred and fifty-five dollars and seventy-seven cents was drawn from the Treasury, leaving unexpended, of the appropriation, eleven thousand two hundred and forty-four dollars and twenty-three cents.

An event which, in more peaceful times, would have excited the liveliest interest throughout the continent, has, owing to our deep solicitude about our domestic concerns, attracted scarcely more than a passing attention. I refer to the completion, in October last, of the Pacific telegraph line, connecting the Atlantic coast with the city of San Francisco. An enterprise of such magnitude, can well be classed among the wonders of the present age. Recognizing this as the forerunner of a railroad, uniting, at no distant day, the same points, and thereby securing an important share of Asiatic commerce to our State, we have special reason for gratulation.

I transmit a copy of the certificate of the Secretary of the Interior, apportioning the representation for the thirty-eighth Congress among the several States, in accordance with the provisions of the act of Congress, approved May 23d, 1850. From this it appears that the State of New York is entitled to thirty-one members in the House of Representatives. It becomes your duty to district the State in conformity with this certificate.

By the Act of Congress of August fifth, 1861, a direct tax of twenty million dollars is laid upon the United States, and apportioned to the States respectively. The proportion of this State is two million six hundred and three thousand nine hundred and eighteen dollars and sixty-six cents. This tax is laid on real estate only. Property belonging to any individual who actually resides thereon, to the value of five hundred dollars, is exempt. The details of the act are quite complex so far as relates to the collection of taxes under it. But it contains a provision that any State may "assume, assess, collect and pay into the treasury of the United States, the direct tax, or its quota thereof, in its own way and manner, by and through its own officers, using a valuation list, made by State authority, and any State giving notice to the Secretary of the Treasury, previous to the second Tuesday of February, shall be entitled, in lieu of all expenses, to a deduction of fifteen per cent. on such portions as have actually been paid into the treasury of the United States on or before the last day of June, and ten per cent. on such parts as shall have actually been paid on or before the last day of September." No assessors or collectors are to be appointed after a State gives notice, and the "quota or direct tax is liable to be paid or satisfied, in whole or in part, by the release of such State advances, duly executed to the United States, of any liquidated and determined claim of such State of equal amount against the United States." I have no hesitation in recommending that the tax be assumed by the State at once; and I submit for your consideration the following mode of liquidating it:

The act of Congress of July twenty-seventh, 1861, provides for indemnifying the States for advances to the General Government, and covers all the expenditures incurred in raising volunteers, under the act of the Legislature of this State, of April 16th.

On the first instant, these amounted in the aggregate to $2,873,501 16
On this, the late Comptroller received from the United States Treasury............................ 1,156,048 50

Leaving still due from the government, on advances, the sum of............................ 1,717,452 66

This balance, it is assumed, will be allowed at the Treasury Department, and will be credited on account of the direct tax due from this State, which, as before stated, is _____ $2,603,918
Deduct the 15 per cent _____ 390,586

Leaving a net tax of _____ $2,213,332
Deduct above balance due on advances of State _____ 1,717,452

And there is found to be due the United States
   Treasury _____ $495,880

Under chapter 277, Laws of 1861, a direct tax of one and a half mills on the taxable property of the State was levied. This will produce about two million one hundred and forty-one thousand dollars, of which but about five hundred thousand dollars, as appears above, will be required to liquidate the balance of the United States tax. It is to be remembered that this State tax was levied upon personal as well as real property, and that there were no exemptions, such as are provided for in the law of Congress. But, with the privilege of adjusting the debt due to the State for advances, the opportunity for making an important saving on the collection of the federal tax, providing at the same time for paying a demand which must be met, the Legislature, I think, will find no difficulty in making such disposition of a part of the proceeds of the tax raised under chapter 277, as will accomplish these ends.

The Act also provides for collecting upon the annual income of every person residing in the United States, whether derived from property or from any profession or vocation, carried on in the United States or elsewhere, if such annual income exceeds eight hundred dollars, a tax of three per centum on the amount of such excess of income above eight hundred dollars, and upon the income, accruing upon any property or securities owned in the United States by any citizen thereof, residing abroad, a tax of five per centum. A favorable exception in both instances is made on income from treasury notes and other securities of the government. These taxes are to be assessed and collected under regulations prescribed by the Secretary of the Treasury.

This is a novelty in our country. We have heretofore taxed only real and personal property. It is obvious that great inequality would result from an enforcement of this law, in a manner so partial as would be the case now. It is understood that Congress will take measures for modifying its provisions. A question as to the constitutionality of this measure has been raised. It is asked if it does not conflict with the terms of section two, article one, United States Constitution, which determines that "representation and taxation shall be apportioned among the several states according to their respective numbers."

In my annual message of 1861, I recommended that the military spirit of the State, which for several years has been gradually declining, should be fostered, and called attention to the fact that it was a part of the established policy of our country to maintain a well regulated militia as a pledge of domestic security, and of safety from external violence. It was obvious that our militia was in no condition, either as respected discipline or equipment, for minute duty. The growing apprehension throughout the country that a collision might occur between the authorities and the insurgents, and especially in view of the fact that our arsenals and armories were lamentably destitute of supplies, induced me on the ninth of January, in transmitting the annual report of the Commissary General, to call special attention to the facts presented therein. Among other things it was shown that the great body of the organized militia of the State was unsupplied with reliable arms. I specially referred to the then existing deficiency in the military stores, which I recommended the Legislature to take early measures to supply, urging that in order to be prepared for any emergency, a suitable appropriation should be made from the Treasury and placed at the discretion of the military department. The favorable terms and the large market at that time, would have enabled the State to procure the necessary articles at very moderate prices when compared with subsequent ones. The final consideration of this subject, as is known, did not take place in the Assembly, until the 12th day of April, when a bill passed appropriating five hundred thousand dollars, for the purpose of arming the militia of the State, and providing for the public defence. There have been purchased in Europe, under this Act, ten thousand Enfield rifled muskets, of which number about six thousand have been delivered in New York. The Report of the Commissary General will embrace a full detail of the receipts and issues of military stores and the present supply of arms and munitions.

Our Constitution requires that the Militia of this State shall at all times be armed and disciplined, and in readiness for service. To accomplish this, some essential modifications of our present militia laws are obviously necessary. As Congress has the power to provide for organizing, arming and disciplining the militia of the country, the system of this State must have for its foundation the various acts of that body. The defective character of the act of Congress of 1792, presents a serious difficulty, in the way of such modifications of our present laws, as experience would dictate. A carefully prepared report, the result of a systematic inquiry and correspondence, with the active military men of the State, made through the Adjutant General, by the Judge Advocate General, will be presented to you. It proposes to retain the main features of the present militia system, to abolish, with two exceptions, the elective system; to return to the mode of enrolling prescribed by the act of 1792, to require yearly drills, and thus provide a well-trained nucleus in every locality; to limit the duration of commissions and to terminate, within a given period, those now in force; to require candidates for commissions to be examined, and the enactment of a series of articles of war, for the government of troops in the service of the State in time of war, based on those in force in the Army. It recommends other and minor amendments. In modifying our system, it is important to keep in view two facts: the one, that too much is not attempted to be accomplished; the other, that suitable provision shall be made for the necessary expenses of the men. The Act of 1792 erred, undoubtedly, in requiring more than it should of a people whose pursuits are largely agricultural and mechanical. Experience shows that those between the ages of twenty and thirty constitute the class, who maintain the militia organizations, and from which has been drawn the great bulk of the volunteers. Upon this class we must principally depend for the efficiency of our future militia establishment.

There is an obvious necessity for immediate attention to this subject, and I therefore recommend the early preparation of a bill, which, while conforming to the laws of Congress, shall meet our present and future needs.

Our political troubles, which have so engrossed the attention and employed the resources of the country since the close of the last session, are the fruits of a tree whose seeds were sown a third of a century ago, and, though unobserved by us, its growth has been carefully watched by those whose nurturing hands have given direction to its roots. The attempt to ignore the Federal power in 1832 was an expression of the same sentiment which now animates the leaders of secession; and time has served to justify the prediction of President Jackson, that, though crushed, the spirit of nullification would revive again under the form of slavery agitation. Slowly, but surely, the process of poisoning the Southern mind has been going forward. History, in its own time, will sit in judgment and review the account: to its record I leave the rise and progress of secession. To those events only which directly involve our duty, shall I refer.

The summer of 1860 was one of peculiar political interest. The manifestations of popular opinion were unusually open and candid. Early in the year political conventions had placed four candidates before the people for the Presidency. Three of these stood unequivocally pledged to uphold the Constitution and maintain the Union. The fourth, while believed by his Northern supporters to be loyal, was, by the more general opinion, regarded as otherwise. Recent events have fully justified the popular suspicion in this respect. The election was on November 6th. The North proceeded calmly and deliberately to the exercise of a right which had been settled at the Revolution and confirmed at every subsequent quadrennial election. The vote was unusually large. The verdict at the polls was emphatic. Of the four million six hundred and fifty-four thousand ballots given, three million eight hundred and fifteen thousand were for unconditional Union. New York, with sixteen others of the thirty-three States, gave her electoral vote for the present incumbent. Aside from the legal obligation, the South, by participating, were bound in honor to accept the result of the election without dissent; but the leaders of disunion, with amazing audacity, made it a pretext for precipitating the catastrophe of attempted secession upon the country. They well knew that the rights of no State had been endangered by the result of the election. Indeed, the successful party had, in all authoritative modes, expressly contended for the right of each State to control its own domestic institutions. More than this, the opposition held a majority in both branches of the National Legislature, and the judiciary, by the Constitution, were a co-ordinate branch of the government and therefore independent of the new administration; besides, the three powers of the government had been, at no period in our history, and, from the nature of things, could never all be held at the same time by either section. The issue of the election gave satisfaction in the city of Charleston, and the result was scarcely made known before the plotters boldly announced their determination to destroy the Union. The leaders would not wait. They dared not. They drove the public assemblies with impetuous haste toward the brink of rebellion. The alleged grievances were but vague generalities. They insulted the national flag at every opportunity; denounced the national government; seized by force and fraud the public property; and repudiated obligations due in loyal States. A firm and clear-sighted Federal Executive would have summarily meted out the penalties of the law to the fomenters of conspiracy and treason. But age and ill-placed confidence had rendered the President timid, and made him blind to obvious facts. Certain members of his Cabinet openly abetted the rebellion, or were guilty of wanton treachery. They used their high positions to strengthen the conspirators and to cripple the army and navy. They had controlled the appointment of diplomatic representatives, placing in important positions those known by them to be inimical to the Government, and secret agents were employed, with their approval, to visit Europe to influence the governing classes there. A legion of evil agencies, some secret, others open, were put to work to demoralize and denationalize the South, a labor rendered practicable by the peculiar character of Southern society. Spurred on by envy and ambition, the leaders toiled like giants. Specious appeals were made to unworthy prejudices. The rankest hostility to Southern interests was imputed to the North. Congress was charged with destroying the commercial equality of the South, and hopes the most extravagant were encouraged. Legislative bodies and conventions of the people were suddenly changed from the object of their convocation; power the most arbitrary was usurped; in a word, the leaders halted at no barrier, and were deterred from no deception, to carry into execution their long concerted scheme of disrupting the Union. A State which had once defied the law, a State which had borne few of the burdens, had had a large hand in shaping the national policy, which had brought weakness rather than strength, and had enjoyed all of the benefits of the Union, was appropriately chosen to lead the way. On the 29th of December, her Legislature passed a formal act of secession. Next followed, in January, Mississippi, Alabama, Florida, Georgia and Louisiana; Texas in February, Virginia in April, and Arkansas, Tennessee and North Carolina in May, making eleven States in all, and seven before the incoming of the new administration. The people of New York, strong in their loyalty and devotion, could not believe that, toward a Government so mild and beneficent as ours, the citizens of any State could seriously entertain a disloyal feeling. They thought that when the ebullitions incident to a general election had subsided, the good sense of the people, would restore harmony. They knew, as all know, that for eighty years the Government had been true to its constitutional obligations, that the immunities of each State had been sacredly observed, and that all alike had enjoyed the unequaled blessings of a truly republican form of government. But the daily proceedings in the rebellious states were such as to create astonishment and to weaken the faith of the most hopeful. Even the President became alarmed at last. On the eighth of January, 1861, in a special message to Congress, in which was exhibited unwonted firmness, he said the Nation was in the midst of a fearful revolution, and reasserted the noble sentiment of the beloved hero who terminated a war, and distinguished the day in our annals, that "the Union must and shall be preserved." He declared his purpose to use the military power against all who resisted the Federal authorities. The Legislature of this State, in a series of resolves, with but three dissenting voices, "hailed with joy the firm, dignified and patriotic special message of the President," and tendered to him whatever aid in men and money he might require, to enforce the laws and uphold the authority of the Federal Government. Copies of these were sent, through me, to the President and to the Governors of all the States.

On the twenty-fourth of January, I received and transmitted to the Legislature, the resolutions adopted four days previously by the General Assembly of Virginia, inviting such States as would "unite with her in an earnest effort to adjust the unhappy controversies, in the spirit in which the Constitution was originally formed and consistently with its principles, so as to afford adequate guaranties to the Slave States for the security of their rights, to appoint commissioners to meet hers, on the fourth of the following month, in Washington, to consider and agree, if practicable, upon some suitable adjustment." Although but eleven days intervened—a period scarcely sufficient even to inform many of the Legislatures in session, and too brief to convene those not in session—I nevertheless, did not feel willing to let this or any opportunity offering a reasonable hope of success, pass without a trial. I accordingly recommended the appointment of five citizens of this State, in whose character and patriotism the public would have full confidence, to meet those from Virginia and other States. On February first, the Legislature selected Commissioners. Their reports will be found in the Senate documents of 1861, numbers fifty-nine and sixty.

On the 21st of March, I received, from the President an authenticated copy of the joint resolutions adopted by Congress proposing an amendment to the Constitution of the United States, which, when ratified by three-fourths of the State Legislatures, should become a part of that instrument, in the following language: "No amendment shall be made to the Constitution which will authorize or give to Congress the power to abolish or interfere, within any State, with the domestic institutions thereof, including that of persons held to labor or service, by the laws of said State." Nothing more than the adoption of this amendment could, in justice, have been asked by the South. It should be remembered that this action was taken after the withdrawal of the representatives of States in rebellion, and this fact alone should have more weight in determining the question of security to Southern rights, and the friendly spirit of the North, than all the assertion and calumny that could be uttered. I transmitted a copy of this to both houses, recommending its adoption. The proposed amendment was not passed upon by them, however.

Events rapidly culminated. The newly organized Confederate administration lost no opportunity to add to the excitement, and to urge on the rebellion. The leaders determined that a "blow must be struck," that "blood must be shed," before their government could have a defined existence. Charleston harbor appeared to be the point selected for this bloody inauguration. The masterly occupation of Fort Sumter by Major Anderson, the prolonged preparations of the insurgents for reducing it, and the firing upon the supply-ship Star of the West, had fixed the eyes of the country upon that point. The peculiar difficulties of affording supplies by a Government vessel, and the meagre amount of subsistence in store, induced the commanding officer to inform the Governor of South Carolina that unless he received a supply in two days he must surrender the fort. As this was obviously impossible, the evacuation by the Federal forces was inevitable. But it did not suit the designs of the rebels to receive the fort without a resort to violence. Without provocation, a cannonade from eleven batteries and a land and water force of more than eight thousand men, opened upon the devoted little band. It was physically impossible for seventy men to hold out against such odds, and the Federal force, under the guns of the rebels, capitulated on the 13th of April. On the same evening, the news flashed over the vast telegraphic net-work of the country. Northern blood was stirred. This gratuitous violence and this deliberate insult to the flag, conclusively proved to all that it was the design of the leaders to break up the Government. An immediate reaction took place in the popular mind, completely uniting the people of the loyal States. They deliberately determined to put down the rebellion, and this purpose has been strengthened by time and reflection. The President immediately appointed a special session of Congress to meet on July the fourth.

He also issued his proclamation, calling for seventy-five thousand three months militia. Of this force the quota of New York was thirteen thousand men. On the morning of the fifteenth, I communicated this fact to the Assembly, and recommended that a military force sufficiently large to meet the present and prospective demands of the Government, be authorized, and that greater discretionary power be conferred to embody and equip a volunteer militia for the public defence, and to provide the necessary means therefor. A bill for this object, in a few hours, passed through all the forms of law, with but six dissenting voices. In the Senate, its passage was equally prompt and decisive. It empowered the Governor, Lieutenant Governor, Secretary of State, Comptroller, State Engineer and Surveyor and State Treasurer, to accept into the service of the State, in addition to and as a part of its militia, for two years, thirty thousand volunteers. The officers named in the Act immediately met and resolved to raise seventeen regiments of seven hundred and eighty men each. A proclamation was issued by me, calling for this force to serve as Infantry or Riflemen, and to rendezvous at New York, Albany and Elmira. As the Board of officers formed under the Act will make a report, accompanied by the minutes of its proceedings, it will be sufficient for me to say that the spirit aroused by the insult to the flag in Charleston harbor sent a company from every neighborhood, and at the end of a fortnight, and just when the spirit of volunteering was rising, the first quota was filled. Through the efforts of a member of the Board, who visited Washington for that purpose, the Government consented to accept the twenty-one regiments still remaining of the force authorized by the Act referred to. On the 16th of April I ordered the Seventh Militia regiment to Washington, and the unprotected condition of that city determined me to dispatch thither at once all the remaining militia strength immediately available. Marching orders were therefore issued to the Sixth, Twelfth and Seventy-First on the 17th, to the Twenty-Fifth on the 19th, and to the Eighth, Thirteenth, Twenty-Eighth and Sixty-Ninth Militia and the Eleventh volunteers on the 20th. It will be remembered that traveling was obstructed on the 20th by the burning of the railroad bridges between Philadelphia and Baltimore. To what extent this fact interfered with the trains, could not be ascertained, as telegraphic communication was cut off almost immediately. I therefore directed the regiments to leave by steamers, by way of the Potomac. The Eleventh volunteers was the only organization raised under the act of April 16th, in any degree ready for service; even that was as yet unorganized, and the election for officers was held on shipboard. It is not improper to say that to the timely arrival of the Militia from this State, must, in a great degree, be ascribed the safety of the Capital and the restoration of security in Washington.

While enlistments were proceeding at a rate altogether unprecedented, the Military Board were employing their energies to supply the necessary clothing and to provide arms. The mercantile class were unprepared for meeting the immediate demands for articles incident to a state of war. So limited was the stock of army cloth in our principal markets, that before any large number of uniforms could be furnished, the wool had to be purchased and the fabric prepared. Through an unfortunate modification of a contract with a respectable firm in the city of New York, for twelve thousand uniforms, a considerable number of suits of very poor quality were delivered to the agents of the State, and before becoming apprized of their inferiority, they were distributed to the troops. The facts respecting this and the terms of settlement with the contractors, will fully appear in the report to which I have referred. It may be proper to add that this circumstance occasioned the greatest vigilance in contracting for and inspecting subsequent supplies of all kinds for our troops.

On the twenty-fourth of April an agent of the State was dispatched to Europe, with a letter of credit for five hundred thousand dollars, and authority to purchase twenty-five thousand stand of arms. On this he obtained and shipped nineteen thousand Enfield muskets, which were delivered in New York at a cost of about three hundred and thirty-five thousand dollars.

By the twenty-fifth of May, the thirty thousand volunteers, authorized by the Act, had been raised, accepted by the Board into the service of the State, and organized into thirty-eight regiments. On the eleventh of June, the respective regimental Field Officers had been elected, and their services accepted, and on the twelfth of July, the last of the thirty-eight regiments had left the State. Thus, in a period of eighty-seven days, a volunteer force of thirty thousand men had been drawn from various parts of the State, organized, fitted for service and dispatched to the seat of war.

There were accepted under authority from the President to a committee of citizens of New York, four Volunteer and four Militia regiments, and according to the best information I have been able to obtain, there were also two other organizations accepted by the War Department, independently of the State authorities, previous to the first of July. By the middle of that month, there were in the service of the Government from this State, of three months militia, about eight thousand three hundred men; of three years militia, about three thousand four hundred; of two years volunteers, thirty thousand; and of three years volunteers, accepted directly by the War Department, and through the committee of citizens of New York, about five thousand, making an aggregate force of forty-six thousand.

Immediately after the engagement at Bull Run, the President communicated to me his desire that New York should furnish an additional force of twenty-five thousand three year volunteers. I promptly informed him of my readiness to aid the Government to any extent it might require, but stated that the power conferred by the Legislature of New York to raise troops for the war was already exhausted, hence it would be necessary for me to convene the Legislature unless the Government would furnish the money necessary for raising, subsisting and equipping this further quota. The latter course met the President's approval. Proper authority was duly granted by the War Department for this purpose, and directions were given to the agents of the Government at Washington, and on service in this State, to aid me in this work. I therefore, on the 25th of

[Assem. No. 2.] 4

July, issued my proclamation, calling for a volunteer force of twenty-five thousand men, to serve for three years or during the war, to rendezvous, as under the first call, at New York, Albany and Elmira. In framing a general order regulating the acceptances of the officers and men, I deemed the good of the service required that all candidates for commissions should pass an examination as to their fitness for field and company officers. The effect of this was, in a partial degree, to retard enlistments, but to give a greatly improved class of officers to the service. At this time, while there was nothing in the aspect of affairs connected with raising men particularly discouraging, yet, owing to several causes, enlistments were less active than they had been. With a view to stimulate volunteering, and at the same time to obtain the best class of troops, I directed the Adjutant General to authorize branch depots in twenty-two different localities, so separated that they would be unlikely to interfere with each other. The objects were more than accomplished. Not only did the change secure a class of troops which for respectability and intelligence can nowhere be surpassed, but it hastened enlistments. Ten regiments have already been raised at these special camps, and a sufficient number of men in addition to these to form eight more.

On October first the Government authorized an increase of the force from this State to one hundred thousand men. Again, on the sixth of November, this number was enlarged to one hundred and twenty-five thousand.

The Annual Report of the Adjutant General will show that New York has sent into the field, of infantry and riflemen, ninety-nine regiments, of which number, eleven were three months militia; of cavalry, ten regiments and one battalion; of artillery, two regiments, two battalions, and nine batteries; a rocket battalion, and a regiment of engineer officers and soldiers; or an organized force equivalent to one hundred and fifteen regiments. In addition to this, there are now in the State, of volunteers mustered into the service of the United States, about fourteen thousand five hundred, or sufficient for fifteen regiments more, increasing New York's contribution to one hundred and thirty regiments.

Muster-in rolls and statistics as to numbers are as yet incomplete, but the accurate returns are not likely to materially vary the following figures relating to the above organizations, namely:

There have left the State in the several regiments, of officers and men	95,078
Recruits since added	11,000
Total that have entered service beyond limits of State	106,078
Now in the State, mustered into U.S. service	14,500
Aggregate number of men raised in State	120,578

Of those who entered the field there have been—

Killed in battle	270
Have died from natural causes	350
Made prisoners of war	550
Honorably discharged	2,700
Discharged by error in U. S. muster	1,500
Discharged by court martial	140
Absent without leave and desertions	3,300
Unaccounted for	900
Discharged by expiration of term of service (3 months militia)	7,334
Now in the field	89,034

If there be added to the latter the volunteers now in the State, an available force of 103,307 is shown.

It is estimated that, in addition to the foregoing aggregate, at least twenty-five hundred men have been drawn from this State and mustered into organizations, not enumerated above.

This force is scattered over nine States, in forty-three different brigades, and under twelve Generals of division.

I will not attempt to heighten the importance of the foregoing exhibit by comments. The figures are more emphatic than words.

The New York troops have taken part in every engagement during the war, east of the Alleghanies and south of Washington. They have enriched the soil of six States with their loyal blood. Their bearing has at all times been that of freemen contending for fireside rights. They have never forgotten the dignity and humanity of the citizen and neighbor in the uniform of the soldier. Courage, coolness, and the endurance of veterans, have characterized them in the hour of danger. Of the first to obey the forward call, one of her young commanders was among the earliest to inscribe his name on the bright page of hero-martyrs. Others, of beloved memory, have fallen; some in battle, others by disease; and not a breeze from the South but bears upon it the manly sighs of others, those who, because they loved and would defend their country's rights, fill the felon's cell. When the enduring record shall be made up, in all that constitutes the brave soldier, the war for the Union will suffer nothing when compared with the grand struggle which gave us a national existence.

On the 28th of September, the President tendered me the appointment of Major General of Volunteers, under the act of Congress of July 25th, 1861, and subsequently created the State of New York into a Military Department, under my command. Finding after a careful examination that there were no constitutional objections to my holding the office, and in view of its practical advantages to the service, I accepted it, although, of course, not intending to receive any of its emoluments.

This summary of facts, connected with meeting the requisitions of the General Government, is respectfully submitted for your information. The Military Board, the Comptroller, and the chiefs of the several staff departments, will present all necessary details. The Legislature will, I am sure, approve the efforts that have been made to meet the demands of the government. The exigency has been great, and the means of providing for it and of meeting in all respects the desires of the public, have at times been beyond the ability of those charged with the duties. If a feeling of impatience has been manifested in consequence, while its influence has been somewhat disheartening upon the public servants, it was but an indication of the deep determination of the people to crush a rebellion, which in all future time will be adjudged the most causeless and most wicked that history records.

Under authority granted from the War Department, contracts have been made by me for large supplies of uniforms, under-clothing, shoes, ordnance stores, equipments, rations, and other necessary supplies for and on account of the United States, and free from any pecuniary liability, except on account of the General Government. I submit a form of the contract, of which several hundred have been executed by me. The uniforms with which our troops are supplied, being more satisfactory to them, and, in certain details, more appropriate than those furnished from the Government store house, I have had the privilege, under authority from the United States, to furnish additional supplies, from time to time, to our troops in the field, so far as practicable, and am glad to say this is a cause of mutual satisfaction to our troops and to the War Department.

Since the last of August, the State has had an agent of much military experience located in the office of the Commissary of Clothing at Washington, through whom our troops were supplied with clothing, and to whom applications for supplies of various kinds could be made. Since the middle of November, the Inspector General of the State has been stationed in that city. His experience in the field, his familiar acquaintance with army officers, and his position on the staff of the Commanding General, have given him peculiar facilities for visiting the camps and inspecting the condition of our regiments and knowing their wants.

It is known to you that the first thirty-eight volunteer regiments were fitted out by the State. Such also was the case with the three months militia. For the remainder of the force, the General Government has furnished, and is to furnish, all the means; and supplies have therefore been in accordance with the general regulations of the Army.

I recommend that an appropriation at once be made for supplying certain articles of comfort rendered very desirable, if not necessary, by the advanced season, which are not provided for by the army regulations, and which, while adding to the comfort of the soldier, will promote the efficiency of the service.

It was not till September that the War Department by a general order gave effect to the Act of Congress of July last, with reference to the allotment by volunteers of portions of their pay for the benefit of their families. Finding that the system was not so generally adopted as it deserved to be, I requested one of the Commissioners to examine the accounts of the Treasurer, &c., to visit the regiments in the field for the purpose of bringing the system to their attention and procuring its adoption to as large an extent as possible. He was directed to state to the volunteers that application would be made to the Legislature to authorize the employment of the Treasury of the State as the depository of the funds so allotted. Before he had completed his labors, Congress, by a new act, placed the matter in the hands of Commissioners appointed by the President, who are to serve without compensation. It is, however, desirable that the Treasurer of the State should be promptly authorized to receive and disburse any portion of their pay that the volunteers may desire. Connected with this, I recommend the adoption of an equitable system of relief to the families of volunteers.

Since the opening of the rebellion I have devoted myself

wholly to the duty in hand, and have earnestly endeavored to preserve the high rank of this State in all matters, and while first regarding the comfort, health and efficiency of the soldier, I have not lost sight of the expenditures involved.

No requisition has been made by the government that remains unhonored. Among the very first to respond to the call for the defence of the Capital in April, New York has not only steadily answered every demand since made, but has time after time besought the privilege of adding to her force in the field. Unless the State shall exhibit an unwillingness to respond to the wishes of the General Government, its constituted authorities would seem to be the proper medium through whom alone company and regimental organizations should be accepted.

On the 19th of October, I received a communication from the Department of State, inviting my consideration of the subject of the improvement and perfection of the harbor defences of the sea and lake coasts of this State, and requesting me to submit the matter to the consideration of the Legislature. Reference was made to the fact, that disloyal persons had hastened to foreign countries even before the present insurrection had revealed itself in arms, to invoke their intervention for the overthrow of the Government and the destruction of the Federal Union, and although unsuccessful in their first efforts, it was believed that those agents were still industriously endeavoring to accomplish their purposes by degrees and by indirection, and were seeking to involve our country in controversies with States, with which every interest requires that it shall remain in relations of peace and friendship.

A personal examination, in company with several competent engineers, led me to call the attention of the Legislature of 1860 to the fact, that the approaches to the city of New York by water were not adequately defended, and the opportunities incidentally afforded me during the past year, fully satisfied me of the insufficiency of our lake defences. I therefore immediately assured the Secretary of State that I would aid the Government in providing for the proper protection of our frontiers and harbor approaches in anticipation of the action of the Legislature. I submit herewith a copy of the correspondence. A preliminary report of the Engineer-in-Chief, relating thereto will be at once transmitted. The subject is one which calls for prompt and effective measures on the part of the Legislature, and I assure you of my cordial co-operation in any plan which will afford entire security to the persons and property of our citizens. I recommend that immediate measures be taken for obtaining from Congress an appropriation sufficient to provide suitable defences at all exposed points; and so that no time shall be lost, I recommend that authority be given to proceed with the work of preliminary survey and to take the proper antecedent steps. In default of the prompt action of the United States authorities, it is manifestly our duty to proceed at once with such portions of the defences as prudence requires, looking to the Government for ultimate reimbursement.

A recent occurrence, which created great solicitude both here and in Europe, and which it was believed by many would lead to hostilities between this country and England, renders it not improper for me to say that no State in the Union has so large an interest as New York in preserving amicable relations, especially with commercial powers. The tonnage and value of vessels owned in the port of New York alone, in 1860, was:

	Tonnage.	Value.
Of sailing vessels	1,258.491	$69,217,005 00
Of steam vessels	205,510	26,716,300 00
Total	1.464,001	$95,933,305 00

The annual average of foreign exports from this State is one hundred and eleven million dollars, and the annual average imports from foreign countries into the State are one hundred and ninety-one million five hundred thousand dollars. The aggregate imports and exports of the port of New York for the year 1860 were three hundred and eighty-four million dollars, or a daily average of foreign commerce exceeding one million of dollars in value passing through the Narrows of New York harbor. The business of the ports would be shown more fully by adding to the above the coasting trade, amounting to double, if not to quadruple, these figures, but there is no official data by which this can be shown. Hostilities with either of the great powers of Europe, and most of all with that government which, from consanguinity, language and customs, is most intimately related to us, would be of untold disaster. No mere pretext, no caprice of court or cabinet, no cause whatever, unless it involve national dignity or we are denied a positive right, could justify the representatives of this State in consenting to a war with foreign powers, especially at a period when extraordinary supplies of men and money have been, and will continue to be, drawn from us, to overwhelm the insurgents at home. We are now engaged in fighting the battle of constitutional freedom, resolved to restore the rightful authority of the Union throughout its whole extent. We are strong, because we are right. We should not weaken ourselves by taking upon us a war of questionable necessity. Our rank upon the waters, and in the family of nations, has been obtained through no aid from others. It must be maintained, as must be all our interests, by ourselves. Our career is just opening, if we preserve our self-respect and the respect of other nations. Let us give no intended offence, and tamely submit to none. We have confidence in the wisdom of the government, and believe that present and prospective questions affecting this country's relations with foreign powers will receive that consideration which their weighty consequences entitle them to, and that the decisions will be founded on principles of law. Their decisions are ours; and in a just cause New York casts everything into the balance. Above and beyond all questions of property, all questions of present ease and present peace, the man of truly American heart rises to maintain the honor of his flag, and to preserve the dignity and stability of his government.

EDWIN D. MORGAN.

Albany, *January* 7, 1862.

DOCUMENTS

ACCOMPANYING THE ANNUAL MESSAGE OF THE
GOVERNOR.

REPORT OF PARDONS *granted during the year 1861, (made in compliance with Art. 4, Sec. 5, of the Constitution).*

Date.	Name of convict.	Crime.	Term of sentence.			Date of sentence.	County of.	Prison.
			Years.	M'ths.	Days.			
Jan. 12	Malona, Rosa	Assault and battery		3		Dec. 10, 1860	Saratoga	Saratoga county jail.
do. 21	Van Kuren, Charles	Grand larceny	2	6		Sept. 21, 1859	Monroe	Auburn.
do. 29	McCarrick, John	Burglary	2			Dec. 9, 1858	Oswego	Auburn.
Feb. 7	Grant, Charles	Perjury	2			Sept. 1, 1859	St. Lawrence	Clinton.
do. 11	Hamilton, Alfred	Forgery	2½			Oct. 17, 1859	Saratoga	Clinton.
do. 20	Garbatiro, Salvadore	Assault with deadly weapon		6		Feb. 11, 1859	New York	Sing Sing.
do. 27	Southworth, George W.	Forgery, 2d degree	10			April 7, 1854	Erie	Auburn.
March 11	Gilman, Calvin	Grand larceny	4			May 22, 1857	Steuben	Auburn.
do. 19	Ryerson, Abra'm, alias Charles, Richmond	Burglary	15			March 1849	New York	Sing Sing.
April 8	King, Calvin, 2d	Rape, burglary and robbery	Life			May 1844	Suffolk	Sing Sing.
do. 24	Plumley, George	Burglary and grand larceny	2			May 30, 1860	Orleans	Auburn.
do. 27	Owens, Richard	Burglary, 3d degree	4	4		April 1858	Albany	Clinton.
May 1	Brennan, Michael	Murder	Life			May 1857	Cayuga	Auburn.
do. 13	Twist, Edward	Burglary	Life			Nov. 24, 1858	Monroe	Monroe county penitentiary.
do. 20	Flint, David	do	5			May 1859	Monroe	Auburn.
do. 20	McCabe, Thomas	Ass't with intent to commit mayhem	2	8		March 1, 1860	Herkimer	Sing Sing.
do. 22	Corcoran, Michael	Burglary	14	6		Oct'r 25, 1849	New York	Sing Sing.
do. 29	Ulrich, Frederick C.	Burglary, 2d degree	6	3		January 1857	Queens	Sing Sing.
June 22	Hurlbert, Dwight	Grand larceny	5			Oct'r 17, 1857	New York	Auburn.
do. 25	Fonda, Isaac H.	Burglary, 3d degree	2			June 1860	Erie	Albany county penitentiary.
do. 29	Noon, Adam	Grand larceny	5	9		June 30, 1859	Albany	Auburn.
do. 29	Burke, John	Robbery, 2d degree	5			June 23, 1859	Erie	Clinton.
July 1	Timm, Patrick	Assault and battery		6		April 30, 1861	Albany	Albany.
do. 9	Orcutt, Harrison	Forgery	5	2		Feb. 16, 1858	New York	Clinton.
do. 13	Giles, Edward	Robbery	10	1		March 12, 1855	Washington	New York penitentiary.
do. 15	Cavanagh, Terrence	Grand larceny	2	6		Dec. 16, 1860	New York	Clinton.
do. 15	Gately, John	Burglary, 3d degree	2	3½		Jan. 25, 1861	New York	New York penitentiary.
do. 29	Powers, James	Petit larceny, 2d offence	2	7		Oct'r 11, 1859	Orange	Clinton.
Aug. 2	O'Neil, Daniel	Robbery, 1st degree	10			April 1856	St. Lawrence	Sing Sing.
do. 2	Pettie, James	Arson, 2d degree	10	6		Oct'r 1855	Tioga	Auburn.

Received	Name	Crime	Yrs.	Mos.	Sentence commenced	County	Prison
Aug. 23	Bostwick, David	Burglary, 1st degree, with intent to commit felony	13		Jan. 15, 1858	Oneida	Auburn.
do 27	Johnson, Mary	Grand larceny	5		June 15, 1857	New York	Sing Sing.
do 27	Dager, George D.	Burglary, 3d degree	3		Feb. 1860	Otsego	Auburn.
do 31	Vaughn, Edward	Grand larceny	3	6	Dec. 21, 1860	Albany	Albany county penitentiary.
Sept. 7	Harrison, Morris	Burglary	4	1	March 1859	Erie	Auburn.
do 9	Ellis, Thomas T.	Grand larceny	4	7	Feb. 20, 1860	New York	Auburn.
do 23	Kline, Andrew	Burglary, 3d degree, and larceny	3	2	Feb. 21, 1860	Oneida	Auburn.
do 23	Robinson, William	Forgery, 2d degree	5		Feb. 22, 1861	New York	New York penitentiary.
do 25	Hart, Matthew }						
	Hart, Patrick } Assault with dangerous weapon	2	2	Feb. 29, 1860	Queens	Sing Sing.
	Hart, Joseph }						
Oct. 4	Kennedy, Robert	Assault and battery	2	4	Aug. 30, 1860	Fulton	Clinton.
do 4	Grant, Lester	Grand larceny	4	6	Jun. 20, 1860	Rensselaer	Clinton.
do 4	Nash, Martin	Burglary	4		Feb. 11, 1858	Saratoga	Clinton.
Nov. 15	Robinson, John	Assault	2	10	Oct'r 10, 1861	New York	New York penitentiary.
do 2	Murphy, Patrick	Manslaughter, 4th degree	1		July 5, 1860	New York	Sing Sing.
do 5	McCulloch, John	Assault and battery	3		Feb. 20, 1861	Albany	Albany county penitentiary.
do 21	Kuarke, James	Larceny	3		April 29, 1859	Albany	Clinton.
do 25	Burns, Charles C.	Grand larceny	4	4	June 6, 1859	Erie	Auburn.
do 27	Devereux, Robert	Grand larceny	4		June 6, 1859	Erie	Auburn.
Dec. 4	Sherlock, Daniel	Burglary	4	4	Dec. 4, 1857	Monroe	Sing Sing.
do 13	Eagan, Helen	Selling liquor without license	2	3	Nov. 25, 1861	Monroe	Monroe county penitentiary.
do 16	Whitlock, George	Robbery	4		Nov. 20, 1860	New York	Sing Sing.
do 17	Glenn, John R.	Bigamy	7	2	March 3, 1860	Albany	Clinton.
do 26	Orr, Hugh	Manslaughter, 2d degree	4		June 21, 1858	Oneida	Auburn.
do 26	Bowman, Richard	Grand larceny	2		June 15, 1858	Erie	Auburn.
do 27	Wilcox, Charles	Larceny	2	6	Oct'r 19, 1861	New York	Sing Sing.
do 31	Sully, James	False pretences	10		April 9, 1860	Erie	Auburn.
do 31	Kennedy, John	Robbery, 1st degree	5		Feb. 9, 1860	Chemung	Auburn.
do 31	Holden, Franklin	Forgery	29		Oct'r 24, 1857	Albany	Clinton.
do 31	Flynn, James	Highway robbery	4		July 9, 1857	New York	Sing Sing.
do 31	O'Sullivan, Patrick	Grand larceny	15		July 7, 1858	Erie	Auburn.
do 31	Wilson, Elizabeth	Grand larceny	10		March 15, 1853	Erie	Sing Sing.
do 31	O'Brien, John	Robbery	10	6	Oct'r 15, 1855	New York	Auburn.
do 31	Griffiths, John	Robbery, 1st degree	10		Nov. 23, 1852	Niagara	Auburn.
do 31	Childs, Benjamin	Bigamy	2	5	Nov. 18, 1859	Monroe	Auburn.

REPORT

Of Commutations granted during the year 1861, (made in compliance with Art. 4, Sec. 5. of the Constitution).

Date of Commutation.	Name of convict.	Convicted of the crime of—	Term of sentence. Years.	M'ths.	Days.	Date of sentence.	Sentenced in county of—	To what prison.	Commuted to—
Jan. 28..	Crapo, James B...	Grand larceny	4	6	....	Oct. 26, 1857	Erie	Auburn	3 years 6 months in Auburn prison.
Feb. 7..	Maroney, Joseph..	Highway robbery	14	4	....	Dec. 8, 1854	Erie	Auburn	6 years 4 months in Auburn prison.
Feb. 8..	Stewarl, Wm......	Assault and battery ...	..	6	....	Nov. 13, 1860	Albany	Albany co. penitent'y..	3 months in Albany co. penitent'y.
March 7..	Loomis, Loren ...	Grand larceny	2	..	....	June 23, 1860	Genesee ...	Auburn	10 months in Auburn prison.
May 8..	Flaherty, Wm. H.	Assault and battery ...	..	6	....	Jan. 16, 1861	Rensselaer..	Albany co. pen....	4 months in Albany co. penitent'y.
May 13..	Filkins, Anthony..	Burglary	4	6	....	Feb. 10, 1859	Oswego....	Auburn	2 years 6 months in Auburn prison.
July 13..	Welch, Wm. E....	Forgery, 2d degree....	10	..	....	April 9, 1856	Albany....	Clinton	6 years in Clinton prison.
Aug. 29..	Winslow, John...	Grand larceny	4	7	....	Nov. 17, 1858	Erie	Auburn	3 years in Auburn prison.
Sept. 20..	Murphy, Dan. J..	Larceny...........	2	..	....	May 15, 1861	New York..	New York pen...	1 year in New York penitentiary.
Sept. 23..	Wooster, Owen....	Petit larceny	..	6	....	June 4, 1861	Onondaga..	Onondaga co. pen...	4 months in Onondaga co. peniten.
Sept. 21..	Myer, John	Burglary and larceny..	4	..	....	Oct. 21, 1858	Wyoming...	Auburn.......	3 years in Auburn prison.
Sept. 25..	Connelly, Thomas.	Burglary, 2d degree...	2	..	....	Dec. 7, 1860	Kings.....	Kings co. pen.....	1 year in Kings co. penitentiary.
Oct. 7..	Daily, John......	Ass't upon public officer	2	..	....	July 9, 1861	Chautauqua	Auburn.......	1 year in Auburn prison.
Oct. 16..	Voght, George H..	Assault with intent to do bodily harm...	2	..	....	Jan. 9, 1861	New York..	Sing Sing	1 year in Sing Sing prison.
Nov. 15..	Connisky, John...	Highway robbery	10	3	....	Feb. 19, 1861	Tioga	Auburn	5 y. 4 m. and 15 d. in Auburn pr.

DEPARTMENT OF THE INTERIOR, WASHINGTON.

To His Excellency EDWIN D. MORGAN,

Governor of the State of New York:

I, Caleb B. Smith, Secretary of the Interior, do hereby certify that, in discharge of the duty devolved on me by the provisions of an act of Congress approved May 23d, 1850, entitled "An act providing for the taking of the Seventh and subsequent Censuses of the United States, and to fix the number of the members of the House of Representatives and provide for their future apportionment among the several States," I have apportioned the Representatives for the Thirty-eighth Congress among the several States, as provided for by said act, in the manner directed by the 25th section thereof.

And I do hereby further certify that the State of New York is entitled to thirty-one (31) members in the House of Representatives for the Thirty-eighth Congress and until another apportionment shall be made according to law.

In testimony whereof, I have hereunto subscribed my name and caused the seal of the Department of the Interior to be
[L. S.] affixed, this 9th day of July, in the year of our Lord, one thousand eight hundred and sixty-one.

(Signed)   CALEB B. SMITH.

DEPARTMENT OF STATE,
WASHINGTON, October 14, 1861.

To His Excellency EDWIN D. MORGAN,

Governor of the State of New York:

SIR:—The present insurrection had not even revealed itself in arms when disloyal citizens hastened to foreign countries to invoke their intervention for the overthrow of the Government and the destruction of the Federal Union. These agents are known to have made their appeals to some of the more important States without success. It is not likely, however, that they will remain content with such refusals. Indeed, it is understood that they are industriously endeavoring to accomplish their disloyal purposes by degrees and by indirection. Taking advantage of the embarrassments of agriculture, manufacture and commerce in foreign countries, resulting from the insurrection they have inaugurated at home, they seek to involve our common country in controversies with States with which every public interest, and every interest of mankind require that it shall remain in relations of peace, amity and friendship. I am able to state for your satisfaction, that the prospect of any such disturbance is now less serious than it has been at any previous period during the course of the insurrection. It is, nevertheless, necessary now, as it has hitherto been, to take every precaution that is possible to avert the evils of foreign war to be superinduced upon those of civil commotion which we are endeavoring to cure. One of the most obvious of such precautions is, that our ports and harbors on the seas and lakes should be put in a condition of complete defence ; for any nation may be said to voluntarily incur danger in tempestuous seasons, when it fails to show that it has sheltered itself on every side from which the storm might possibly come.

The measures which the Executive can adopt in this emergency, are such only as Congress has sanctioned, and for which it has provided. The President is putting forth the most diligent efforts to execute these measures, and we have the great satisfaction of seeing that these efforts, seconded by the favor, aid and support of a loyal, patriotic and self-sacrificing people, are rapidly bringing the military and naval forces of the United States into the highest state of efficiency. But Congress was chiefly absorbed, during its recent extra session, with those measures, and did not provide as amply as could be wished. for the fortification of our sea and lake coasts. In previous wars, loyal States have applied themselves by independent and separate activity, to support and aid the Federal Government in its arduous responsibilities. The same disposition has been manifested in a degree eminently honorable, by all the loyal States, during the present insurrection. In view of this fact, and relying upon the increase and continuance of the same disposition on the part of the loyal States, the President has directed me to invite your consideration to the subject of the improvement and perfection of the defences of the State over which you preside, and to ask you to submit the subject to the consideration of the Legislature when it shall have assembled. Such proceedings by the State would require only a temporary use of its means. The expenditures ought to be made the subject of conference with the Federal authorities. Being thus made with the concurrence of the Government, for general defence, there is every reason to believe that Congress would sanction what the State should do, and would provide for its reimbursement.

Should these suggestions be accepted, the President will direct proper agents of the Federal Government to confer with you, and to superintend, direct and conduct the prosecution of the system of defence of your State.

I have the honor to be, sir, your obedient servant,

WILLIAM H. SEWARD.

———

EXECUTIVE DEPARTMENT, }
ALBANY, *Oct.* 19, 1861. }

SIR :—I have this day received your letter of the 14th instant, on the subject of the improvement and perfection of the port and harbor defences of this State, and asking my consideration of its suggestions and desiring the subject to be submitted by me to the Legislature, when it shall have assembled.

I fully appreciate the importance of your recommendations, and shall most cordially aid in carrying out the policy of the Government, in this regard. I feel that we are admonished by the lessons of the year to rely upon our ability to preserve and protect our rights, and not upon the supposed interest, or the presumed friendship of others.

The State of New York, considering the importance of her principal seaport and the extent of her northern lake-bound frontier, is deeply interested in strengthening, and, if necessary, increasing our national defences. Although we may have no present means in our treasury applicable to the expense, and our Legislature does not meet until January next, I have, nevertheless, called to my council Colonel Richard Delafield, of the U. S. Corps of Engineers, for the purpose of considering and adopting the measures demanded by the importance of the subject. He will report here on Monday. I shall direct him, and such other competent and proper gentlemen as may be associated with him, to proceed at once to an examination into the condition of our border defences, especially at the lake ports, and will, at the earliest moment, communicate to you the result, together with such views of my own on the subject as may seem justified by the facts developed by and the circumstances then existing.

I have the honor to be, with high regard,

Your obedient servant,

E. D. MORGAN, *Governor of New York.*

Honorable WM. H. SEWARD, *Secretary of State,*

Washington, D. C.

Hon. WM. H. SEWARD, *Sec'y of State:*

SIR—I had the honor, on the 19th ultimo, to acknowledge your favor of the 14th of that month, in relation to the subject of the improvement and perfection of the defences of this State. I stated in substance that I would take immediate steps to procure some needed information (which has since been obtained), and that I would, at an early day, again communicate with you. I have deliberately considered the subject to which your communication relates and I do approve the suggestions made therein, and I shall be pleased to have the President designate some officer, who will act as an agent of the Government, and with whom I can immediately and directly confer preparatory to prosecuting a system of defence in this State.

I have the honor to be, with high regard,

Your obedient servant,

E. D. MORGAN, *Governor of New York.*

DEPARTMENT OF STATE,
WASHINGTON, *November* 11, 1861.

To His Excellency EDWIN D. MORGAN,
Governor of the State of New York, Albany:

SIR—I have the honor to acknowledge receipt of your Excellency's reply to a circular letter which I addressed to you, on the subject of defences within your State, and to inform you that the correspondence has been referred by the Department of War, to the Military Engineers.

I am, sir, your obedient servant,

WILLIAM H. SEWARD.

EXECUTIVE DEPARTMENT,
ALBANY, *November* 15, 1861.

GENERAL—In acknowledging the communication of the Hon. the Secretary of State, under date of the 14th ultimo, I expressed the desire to co-operate with the Government, or to carry into effect the measures proper to put in a condition of complete defence, the ports and harbors of this State, on the sea and lakes, requesting at the same time, in conformity with the suggestions of the Secretary of State, that the Government would select a proper agent to confer with me in relation to a system of defence.

In reply to this letter, Mr. Seward informed me, under date of the 11th instant, that the correspondence on this subject had been referred, by the Department of War, to the Military Engineers.

After receiving the first letter from the State Department, I directed a preliminary examination to be made into the condition of the fortifications, the amount of ammunition on hand, &c.; and also a partial examination of the lake defences, but as the information in your possession is, undoubtedly, more complete than that obtained by me, I deem it unnecessary to transmit, at this time at least, the result of this inquiry, particularly as I am unadvised as to the course you have determined to pursue.

No State is more deeply interested than New York in securing a thorough system of defences, which, it must be admitted, are, at this time, in a very imperfect and unsatisfactory condition; and I beg to assure you of my readiness to co-operate with the Government, and especially with your Department, in whatever measure is necessary to perfect them. Awaiting your reply,

I have the honor to be, your most ob'd't servant,

E. D. MORGAN, *Governor of New York.*

Brig. Gen. Jos. G. TOTTEN,
Chief of Engineers, Washington, D. C.

ENGINEERS' DEPARTMENT,
WASHINGTON, *November* 27, 1861.

His Excellency Governor E. D. MORGAN, *Albany, N. Y.:*

SIR—On my return from an absence of some continuance, I find your letter of 15th inst., relating to the circular of the Hon. Secretary of State of 14th ultimo.

The subject is now under consideration by me, and I shall have the honor of responding to your communication with the least delay possible.

I have the honor to be, very respectfully,

Your ob'd't servant,

JOS. G. TOTTEN,
Bt. Brig. Gen'l and Civil Engineer.

EXECUTIVE DEPARTMENT,
ALBANY, *December* 18, 1861.

GENERAL—On the 15th of November, I had the honor of addressing you on the subject of the port and harbor defences of this State.

As I then said the Honorable the Secretary of State had invited my co-operation with the Government, in carrying into effect proper measures for putting into a condition of complete safety, the lake and sea ports of this State. I immediately assured him of my great willingness to aid in the matter to any required extent, and requested that a proper agent of the Government might be selected to confer with me in relation to a system of defences as had been proposed by him. In his reply, Mr. Seward informed me that the correspondence on the subject, had been referred by the Department of War, to the Military Engineers. I then wrote you as above stated. In your answer under date of the 27th ultimo, you informed me that you would respond to my communication without unnecessary delay. I had also the honor of a personal interview with you on a late visit to Washington.

The exposed situation of this State by sea and lake, renders our citizens apprehensive of danger on the least appearance of it. The recent affair of the Trent, and the possible consequences growing out of it has caused much solicitude in the city of New York, especially in commercial circles, along the borders of the lakes and at points where it is thought the canals might be damaged, and sources of supplies of water could be cut off.

I earnestly desire to co-operate with you, in taking such immediate preliminary steps as shall re-assure all classes and give them to feel that no time will be lost, nor means be spared by the authorities to protect the interests of the citizens.

The Honorable William A. Dart, United States District Attorney for the Northern District of New York, will present this letter to you, and will confer personally with you. Be pleased to give him such information as will enable me to take early action in relation to the subject I have referred to.

I have the honor to be, with high regard, your ob't serv't,

E. D. MORGAN.

Brigadier General J. G. Totten, *Chief of Engineers, &c.,*

Washington, D. C.

ENGINEER DEPARTMENT,   }
WASHINGTON, *December* 24, 1861. }

His Excellency Governor MORGAN, *Albany:*

Sir—I had the honor to receive, yesterday, your telegram, dated that day, and to immediately acknowledge, by telegraph, its receipt as well as that of your letter by Mr. Dart, and to state that I am busily engaged in a report to your Excellency on the fortifications, which would have been sent earlier but for duties not to be set aside.

Very respectfully, your obedient servant,

JOS. G. TOTTEN,

Brevet Brig. Gen'l and Civil Engineer.

FORM OF CONTRACTS.

THIS AGREEMENT, made and entered into this day of , in the year of our Lord, one thousand, eight hundred and sixty by and between EDWIN D. MORGAN, Governor of the State of New York, for, and in behalf of, the United States of America, under the authority of an order of the Secretary of War, bearing date August 3d, 1861, and of subsequent orders, party of the first part, and

of part of the second part witnesseth, that the said party of the first part, in behalf of the United States of America, as aforesaid, and the said part of the second part, for heirs, executors and administrators, have covenanted and agreed, and by these presents do mutually covenant and agree, as follows, to wit :

First.—That the said shall and will furnish and deliver unto the said party of the first part, at such rations or board, at the option of the party of the first part, as may be required for the use of the New-York State Volunteers raised, or to be raised, for the United States service, together with comfortable lodging and quarters, commencing on the day of and ending on such day as the party of the first part, or any duly authorized officer or agent of said party of the first part, shall direct, at the price of for each complete ration in the raw state, and at the price of for the board each day of each man three meals per day, and in the proportion of one-third of said price for each meal, when such board is furnished, cooked and served as hereinafter provided, without extra charge for said lodging and quarters, whether raw or cooked rations are furnished as aforesaid.

Second.—That the raw ration to be furnished under this contract shall consist of the following articles, to wit:—Three-fourths of a pound of pork or bacon, or one and a fourth pounds of fresh or salt beef; eighteen ounces of bread or flour, or twelve ounces of hard bread, or one and one-fourth pounds of corn meal; and at the rate to one hundred rations of eight quarts of beans, or in lieu thereof, twice per week, one hundred and fifty ounces of desiccated potatoes, and one hundred ounces of mixed vegetables; ten pounds of coffee, or in lieu thereof, one and one-half pounds of tea; fifteen pounds of sugar, four quarts of vinegar, one pound of sperm candles, or one and one-fourth pounds of adamantine candles, or one and one-half pounds of tallow candles; four pounds of soap and two quarts of salt; and in all cases where articles of one kind are permitted or provided, as above, in lieu of other articles, the kinds, quantities and proportions of such several articles from time to time required, shall be entirely under the control and direction of the party of the first part.

Third.—The provisions and other articles stipulated to be furnished under this contract, shall be of the first and best quality, and the food provided for each man, where board is furnished, shall be in all cases, and at all times, equal in quantity and quality, and all other respects, to the raw ration above specified; and said food shall be cooked, prepared and served in a cleanly, healthful and proper manner, with the coffee or tea mentioned in the rations duly prepared for drinking; and the necessary utensils for cooking and eating shall be furnished by said part   of the second part.

Fourth.—In case board is furnished, the said part   of the second part will furnish soap and candles in proportions as above; and in every case the soap and candles will be delivered in bulk to the order of a duly authorized officer of the party of the first part, for distribution by him: where gas, or other sufficient light is provided, said candles need not be furnished.

Fifth.—This contract, and all obligations of the party of the first part thereunder, may at any time be terminated by the said party of the first part, or a duly authorized officer of the said party of the first part, by a written notice to said part   of the second part.

Sixth.—The party of the first part, in behalf of the United States as aforesaid, doth hereby agree to pay for the rations and board, so furnished as aforesaid, at the rates above specified, payments to be due monthly, and to be made according to the terms of said order of the Secretary of War, dated August 3d, 1861, and the order supplementary thereto, bearing date August 8th, 1861, and of subsequent orders, and in the manner and at the times when the United States, in accordance with said orders, shall furnish funds for the payment of the same; which said orders are expressly referred to and made part of this Agreement, the same as if set forth at length herein, without any liability on the part of the State of New York, or of the said Edwin D. Morgan, individually, in the premises, which is hereby expressly waived by said part of the second part.

Seventh.—It is understood and agreed, that this contract is not assignable by the part   of the second part without permission of the party of the first part; and in case of such assignment without such permission, the party of the first part may regard the same as an abandonment of this Agreement, and the said part   of the second part and sureties shall thereupon be held responsible for any loss or damage in the premises.

Eighth.—No member of Congress shall be admitted to any share or part in this contract, or in any benefit to arise therefrom.

In witness whereof, the parties to these presents have hereunto set their hands and seals the day and year first above written.

Sealed and delivered in presence of

[L. S.]

[L. S.]

STATE OF NEW YORK, } ss.
County of

On this   day of   in the year of our Lord one thousand eight hundred and sixty   , before me came the above named   to me known to be the individuals described in, and who executed, the aforegoing instrument, and severally acknowledged to me that they had executed the same, the said Edwin D. Morgan acknowledging the same in behalf of the United States.

Know all Men by these Presents, That we   of   and   of   are held and firmly bound unto The United States of America in the sum of   dollars, lawful money of the United States of America, for which payment well and truly to be made, we bind ourselves, our heirs, executors and administrators, jointly and severally, firmly, by these presents. Sealed with our seals.

[Assem. No. 2.]   G

Dated the   day of   in the year of our Lord one thousand eight hundred and sixty

The condition of this obligation, which is assumed by the obligors in consideration of the sum of one dollar, and of the execution of the articles of agreement hereinafter mentioned, is such, that if   shall and do in all things well and truly observe, perform, fulfill, accomplish and keep, all and singular, the covenants, conditions and agreements which on   part are, or ought to be, observed, performed, fulfiled and accomplished, comprised and mentioned in certain Articles of Agreement bearing date the   day of   between Edwin D. Morgan, Governor of the State of New York, in behalf of the United States, on the one part, and the said   on the other part, according to the true intent and meaning thereof, then, and in that case, the above obligation to be void, otherwise to remain in full force and virtue.

Sealed and delivered in presence of

STATE OF NEW YORK, } ss.
County of

On this   day of   186   before me came the above named   and both to me known to be the same individuals described in, and who executed, the aforegoing instrument, and severally acknowledged to me that they had executed the same.

STATE OF NEW YORK, } ss.
County of

being severally duly sworn, do depose and say, and each for himself deposeth and saith, that he is a freeholder in the State of New York, and is worth the sum of   dollars, over and above all his debts and liabilities, and not including property exempt by law from execution.

Sworn to before me, this
day of   186   }